Happy Kids

CRAFT AND COLOR DESIGNS

by Annie Lang

Ready to use timeless designs and fun for all ages!

You'll find 21 full page vividly colored whimsical designs chosen
from Annie Lang's most popular character images library
to use for your creative DIY projects You'll also find the line art
patterns for each of the designs that you can trace, transfer and
color any way you please. Whether it's a tote bag, wearables,
canvas art or papercrafts, the sky's the limit when you work with
professional designs and patterns. So go ahead and get
your Creative Adventures started and we'll share a few smiles
along the way!

Copyright (C) Annie Lang 2018 anniethingspossible.com
The images in this book are intended for personal, classroom and small resale
business use to create individually crafted items.   Use for the creation
of commercially manufactured/printed product items is strictly prohibited.
Content in this publication. may not be duplicated or distributed for the purpose
of electronic data file sharing either for free or for profit. Annie Lang retains
all rights to the copyrighted properties in this publication and rights to any
images cannot be claimed, reassigned or transferred to another party.

Transferring the linework designs

Trace the design of your choice with pencil and tracing paper.
Place transfer paper under the tracing paper and place onto
your selected surface. Hold in place with tape if necessary.
Retrace over the linework to transfer the design onto the project.
For fabrics, trace the design, flip the pattern over and retrace
the lines using a fabric transfer pen. Follow manufacturer's
direction to iron the design onto your chosen fabric item.

Color or paint these designs with

Craft paints, watercolors, markers, coloring pencils, chalks,
inks, fabric pens, paint pens, or crayons

These designs are great for

Home Dec Items like furniture, cabinets, accent items, walls,
lamps, glassware, kitchen accessories, office and desk items,
bathroom accents, cabinets, patio pots and outdoor items, etc.
Fabric and wearable items like t-shirts, sweatshirts, aprons,
canvas shoes, totes, quilting squares, table linens and napkins,
window and shower curtains, pillows, etc.
Paper Craft Projects like greeting cards, scrap page elements,
tags, labels, stationery items, ornaments, gift bags, etc.

For more ideas and designer tips, please visit my Blog at

http://annielang-anniethingspossible.blogspot.com/
My Pinterest Board at http://www.pinterest.com/anniethings/
or my Facebook Page at
http://www.facebook.com/anniethingspossible

Let's Make Something FUN!

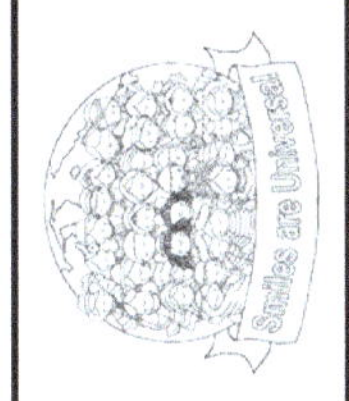

GIMME A SMILE

GIMME A SMILE

(C) Annie Lang anniethingspossible.com

CAMPING

(C) Annie Lang anniethingspossible.com

(C) Annie Lang anniethingspossible.com

(C) Annie Lang anniethingspossible.com

(C) Annie Lang anniethingspossible.com

Cowboys
have more
FUN!
(C) Annie Lang anniethingspossible.com

(C) Annie Lang anniethingspossible.com

(C) Annie Lang anniethingspossible.com

(C) Annie Lang anniethingspossible.com

Fishing Buddy

(C) Annie Lang anniethingspossible.com

(C) Annie Lang anniethingspossible.com

Fishing Buddy

(C) Annie Lang anniethingspossible.com

Fishing Buddy

(C) Annie Lang anniethingspossible.com

(C) Annie Lang anniethingspossible.com

(C) Annie Lang anniethingspossible.com

(C) Annie Lang anniethingspossible.com

(C) Annie Lang anniethingspossible.com

(C) Annie Lang anniethingspossible.com

(C) Annie Lang anniethingspossible.com

(C) Annie Lang anniethingspossible.com

(C) Annie Lang anniethingspossible.com

(C) Annie Lang anniethingspossible.com

(C) Annie Lang anniethingspossible.com

(C) Annie Lang anniethingspossible.com

(C) Annie Lang anniethingspossible.com

(C) Annie Lang anniethingspossible.com

(C) Annie Lang anniethingspossible.com

TOTALLY AMAZING SUPERSTAR

(C) Annie Lang anniethingspossible.com

(C) Annie Lang anniethingspossible.com

(C) Annie Lang anniethingspossible.com

(C) Annie Lang anniethingspossible.com

(C) Annie Lang anniethingspossible.com

(C) Annie Lang anniethingspossible.com

(C) Annie Lang anniethingspossible.com

(C) Annie Lang anniethingspossible.com

(C) Annie Lang anniethingspossible.com

(C) Annie Lang anniethingspossible.com

(C) Annie Lang anniethingspossible.com

(C) Annie Lang anniethingspossible.com

www.ingramcontent.com/pod-product-compliance
Lightning Source LLC
Chambersburg PA
CBHW040146240726
48664CB00002B/616